T0403214

COUNTRIES

FRANCE

by Samantha S. Bell

Focus Readers
NAVIGATOR

WWW.FOCUSREADERS.COM

Copyright © 2025 by Focus Readers®, Mendota Heights, MN 55120. All rights reserved. No part of this book may be reproduced or utilized in any form or by any means without written permission from the publisher.

Focus Readers is distributed by North Star Editions:
sales@northstareditions.com | 888-417-0195

Produced for Focus Readers by Red Line Editorial.

Content Consultant: Maxence Leconte, PhD, Assistant Professor of French Studies, Trinity University

Photographs ©: Shutterstock Images, cover, 1, 4–5, 11, 13, 14–15, 16, 19, 20–21, 23, 25, 26–27; Red Line Editorial, 7; iStockphoto, 8–9; Chesnot/Getty Images Entertainment/Getty Images, 29

Library of Congress Cataloging-in-Publication Data
Names: Bell, Samantha, author.
Title: France / by Samantha S. Bell.
Description: Mendota Heights, MN: Focus Readers, [2025] | Series: Countries | Includes index. | Audience: Grades 4-6
Identifiers: LCCN 2024035796 (print) | LCCN 2024035797 (ebook) | ISBN 9798889982227 (hardcover) | ISBN 9798889982784 (paperback) | ISBN 9798889983842 (pdf) | ISBN 9798889983347 (ebook)
Subjects: LCSH: France--Juvenile literature.
Classification: LCC DC17 .B45 2025 (print) | LCC DC17 (ebook) | DDC 944--dc23/eng/20240807
LC record available at https://lccn.loc.gov/2024035796
LC ebook record available at https://lccn.loc.gov/2024035797

Printed in the United States of America
Mankato, MN
012025

ABOUT THE AUTHOR
Samantha S. Bell lives in the foothills of the Blue Ridge Mountains with her family and lots of cats. She is the author of more than 150 nonfiction books for kids from kindergarten through high school. She loves learning about the different countries and cultures that are part of our amazing world.

TABLE OF CONTENTS

CHAPTER 1
Welcome to France 5

CHAPTER 2
History 9

CHAPTER 3
Climate, Plants, and Animals 15

CLIMATE CRISIS IN FRANCE
Heat and Rain 18

CHAPTER 4
Resources, Economy, and Government 21

CHAPTER 5
People and Culture 27

Focus Questions • 30
Glossary • 31
To Learn More • 32
Index • 32

CHAPTER 1

WELCOME TO FRANCE

France is the third-largest country in Europe. It shares borders with several other countries. France's natural landscape makes up some of these borders. The Rhine River forms part of the border with Germany. The Pyrenees mountains form the border with Spain. And the Alps form the border with Italy.

The French city of Strasbourg is located near the Rhine River.

Some areas of France have flat plains. Others have rolling hills. The flat and hilly areas are in the west and north. Other parts of the country are mountainous. Many of these areas are in the south and east.

Paris is the capital of France. More than two million people live there. Paris also gets more visitors than any other French city. Many tourists go to Nice, too. Nice is by the Mediterranean Sea. The coastal area is called the French Riviera. People enjoy its blue water and sandy beaches.

Many French cities are very old. For example, Romans founded Lyon in the first century BCE. People first lived in Marseille around 600 BCE. It was a Greek **colony**. France's long history and beautiful landscapes add to its fascinating culture.

MAP OF FRANCE

CHAPTER 2

HISTORY

Thousands of years ago, people known as the Celts lived in France. These people lived in small communities. They hunted and farmed on the land. In the first century BCE, Romans arrived. The Romans named the area Gaul. They held control for hundreds of years.

Ancient Romans built structures such as the Pont du Gard in southern France to transport water.

In the 400s CE, the Franks came to Gaul. Like the Celts, Franks lived in small tribes. Each tribe had its own leader. Around 500 CE, that changed. A leader called Clovis I united the tribes. He became king of one large kingdom. But the kingdom did not last long. Soon, the area was divided again.

Around 1000 CE, strong leaders began uniting the Franks again. The new kingdom was called France. It used a **feudal system**. Rich, powerful people owned much of the land. Most other people were poor farmers. They worked on the richer people's land. In return, the richer people protected the farmers.

Remains of buildings from the feudal period can still be seen around France.

In 1337, France went to war against England. The war lasted until 1453. It became known as the Hundred Years' War. France won the war. It was a major victory for the kingdom. People began to feel proud of being French.

Another major change came in 1789. Many French people were not happy with the **monarchy**. So, they overthrew the rulers. Then they formed a new government. The new government did not have a king. Instead, the people would choose their leaders. But this government didn't last long. In 1799, Napoleon

JOAN OF ARC

Joan of Arc is a famous figure in French history. She was born during the Hundred Years' War. Joan was the daughter of a French farmer. When she was 13 years old, she said God was sending her messages. So, Joan cut her hair. She put on armor. Then she led 4,000 soldiers into battle. They defeated the English.

The Palace of Versailles was home to France's royal family starting in 1682.

Bonaparte took control. He became the first French **emperor**.

In 1815, Napoleon was defeated. A new king came to the throne. The changes did not end there. Over the next century, control of France continued to shift. Finally, in 1958, a new **republic** began.

CHAPTER 3

CLIMATE, PLANTS, AND ANIMALS

France's regions have different climates. In the west, summers are cool. Winters are mild. Central and eastern France are more extreme. They have hotter summers and colder winters. The south has dry summers and rainy winters. The mountainous areas receive the heaviest rain and snow.

Mont Blanc is one of the tallest mountains in Europe. Its top is usually snowy.

15

Chamois live in the French Alps.

France is home to many kinds of plants. Small grasses and wildflowers grow in the mountainous regions. Vines and fruit grow near the Mediterranean Sea. Much of the country is forested. High in the mountains, spruce and mountain pine trees are common. Oak, beech, and chestnut trees grow in lower areas.

The country has many types of animals, too. Wild boars live near villages in the countryside. Red deer live in the forests. France has many kinds of snails. More than 30 of those kinds are **endangered**.

PINK VISITORS

Every year, thousands of flamingos fly to southern France. The flamingos visit the salty marshes there. Pink algae live in the marsh water. The flamingos eat the algae. That turns the flamingos' feathers pink. Later, the flamingos move on. They fly down to warmer areas farther south.

CLIMATE CRISIS IN FRANCE

HEAT AND RAIN

Climate change threatens many areas of France. In some cases, climate change leads to extreme weather events. These events can cause serious damage. For example, warming temperatures create heat waves. People and wildlife suffer. People may even die from the heat. More than 5,000 people lost their lives in a heat wave in 2022.

Heat waves are most common in summer. But recently, heat waves in France have been coming later, too. That often harms the country's plants. Many trees don't get enough water. They dry up. That increases the risk of wildfires. Longer heat waves are also bad for farms. Farmers can't produce as much food.

Sometimes, climate change can cause too much rain. In many cases, warm weather makes the rain **evaporate**. That means there is extra

In 2016, flooding in some parts of France was the worst in 100 years.

water in the air. The process can cause powerful storms to develop. These storms often cause heavy flooding in France. Floods damage homes, roads, and bridges. They can harm farmland as well.

CHAPTER 4

RESOURCES, ECONOMY, AND GOVERNMENT

France has many natural resources. The country has great land for farming. Farmers grow wheat, sugar beets, and corn. France also produces dairy products. People around the world love France's cheeses.

Forests are another natural resource in France. People use the trees for wood

Bordeaux is in southwestern France. It is an excellent place for growing grapes.

21

products. Other resources come from under the earth. People mine metals such as nickel, copper, and aluminum.

France's energy sources include coal, natural gas, and oil. France creates energy from moving water, too. **Nuclear energy** is another major type. France is the second-largest nuclear energy producer in the world.

Tourism is a key part of France's economy. Millions of people work in jobs related to tourism. Visitors also bring money into the country. They travel to cities such as Paris and Nice. Visitors spend money at hotels, restaurants, and shops.

France gets more than two-thirds of its electricity from nuclear power.

France also exports many goods to other countries. The country's perfumes are famous. So are makeup and fashion brands. Other products include medicines and parts for airplanes.

23

France's government has three branches. The first is the executive branch. The president leads this branch. French people vote to choose their president.

The French Parliament is France's legislative branch. It has two parts. The National Assembly is one. It passes and changes laws. People elect the National Assembly members. The other part of Parliament is the Senate. Its members are not elected. National Assembly members and other government officials choose them. Senate members defend the interests of different regions and organizations.

The French Senate meets in the Luxembourg Palace in Paris.

The third part of France's government is the judicial branch. This branch decides what laws mean. It includes courts and judges.

CHAPTER 5

PEOPLE AND CULTURE

France is a diverse country. The country's official language is French. However, people use different versions of the language. These versions vary by region. People speak other languages in France, too. Common languages include German, Flemish, and Arabic.

The Grand Mosque of Paris is one of the country's largest mosques.

27

Many **immigrants** settle in France each year. They bring new languages and customs. Many people come from North African countries that France colonized in the past. Algeria, Morocco, and Tunisia are some of the most common.

Food is an important part of daily life for most people in France. People focus on enjoying food with friends and family.

THE LOUVRE

The Louvre is in Paris. It is the world's largest art museum. More than seven million people visit each year. Visitors come to see many famous pieces of art. One example is the *Mona Lisa*. Leonardo da Vinci painted the piece in the early 1500s. The Louvre also has famous sculptures such as the *Venus de Milo*.

The *Mona Lisa* is one of France's most famous art pieces.

Art is important to French culture, too. In the early 1900s, Paris attracted artists from around the world. Today, Paris is still one of the top locations for art museums. France's history and culture are respected around the world.

FOCUS QUESTIONS

Write your answers on a separate piece of paper.

1. Write a few sentences about the main ideas of Chapter 4.

2. What part of French history do you find most interesting? Why?

3. When did Napoleon Bonaparte take control of France?
    - **A.** 1337
    - **B.** 1799
    - **C.** 1958

4. How could flooding in France harm farmlands?
    - **A.** Plants grow too quickly when it floods.
    - **B.** Too much water drowns the plants.
    - **C.** Flooding makes the plants taste worse.

Answer key on page 32.

GLOSSARY

climate change
A human-caused global crisis involving long-term changes in Earth's temperature and weather patterns.

colony
An area controlled by a country that is far away.

emperor
A ruler who controls a group of nations or territories.

endangered
In danger of dying out.

evaporate
To change from a liquid to a gas.

feudal system
A system in which poorer people work the land for wealthy landowners.

immigrants
People who move to a new country.

monarchy
A system of government in which a king or queen rules.

nuclear energy
Power produced by splitting tiny bits of matter called atoms.

republic
A country governed by elected leaders.

TO LEARN MORE

BOOKS
Haley, Charly. *Your Passport to France*. North Mankato, MN: Capstone Press, 2021.

Layton, Christine. *Travel to France*. Minneapolis: Lerner Publications, 2024.

Nnachi, Ngeri. *Spotlight on France*. Minneapolis: Lerner Publications, 2024.

NOTE TO EDUCATORS
Visit **www.focusreaders.com** to find lesson plans, activities, links, and other resources related to this title.

INDEX

Alps, 5, 7
art, 28–29

Bonaparte, Napoleon, 12–13

Celts, 9–10
climate change, 18–19

feudal system, 10
Franks, 10
French Riviera, 6–7

Gaul, 9–10
government, 12–13, 24–25

Hundred Years' War, 11–12

immigrants, 28

Louvre, 28

Marseille, 7

Nice, 6–7, 22
nuclear energy, 22

Paris, 6–7, 22, 28–29
Pyrenees, 5, 7

resources, 21–22
Rhine River, 5

wildlife, 17–18